ARFOOT
OOTH
SAMPSON&BARFOOT
HORSE
&
MEDICINES
OF EVERY
DESCRIPTION
DRUGS
SUNDRIES,
PERFUMERY
&c
PAINTS
OILS
VINEGARS
&c
DRUGGISTS
CHEMISTS

BRITAIN
IN OLD PHOTOGRAPHS

CHESTERFIELD

PAST & PRESENT

BRIAN DAVIS

Sutton Publishing Limited
Phoenix Mill · Thrupp · Stroud
Gloucestershire · GL5 2BU

First published 2003

Title page photograph: Low Pavement, early
twentieth century.
Endpapers: The south-eastern corner of Market
Place past and present.

British Library Cataloguing in Publication Data
A catalogue record for this book is available from the
British Library.

ISBN 0-7509-3125-6

Typeset in 10.5/13.5 Photina.
Typesetting and origination by
Sutton Publishing Limited.
Printed and bound in England by
J.H. Haynes & Co. Ltd, Sparkford.

Three interesting forms of transport line up at Crich Tramway Museum, 2002.

CONTENTS

The Royal Oak, 2002.

INTRODUCTION

I have always been a keen photographer, but I had not considered doing a book on Chesterfield until Sutton Publishing approached me. Initially I thought it would be an easy exercise but as I worked at the project I began to realise what a mammoth task it was. As well as taking all of the 'Now' photographs, which I enjoyed, I needed to research what was available for the 'Thens'. . . . However, I have been a member of Chesterfield Photographic Society for many years, and the annual exhibitions have often included paired photographs of Chesterfield old and new, so this gave me a starting point. Nevertheless, as I progressed with the project it grew bigger and bigger until it became more a matter of what to leave out.

During my work in taking the new photographs, I met a lot of friendly people who gave me plenty of help and advice. I carried around a file of the old photographs to assist me in finding the right spot to take the new ones. Those old photographs were frequently the key to opening the door to further information, as everyone wanted to see the old shots; there is a peculiar fascination in seeing familiar places as our great-grandparents would have seen them.

Undertaking the project has also given me opportunities to go behind the scenes at the hospital and to fly over the town in a light aircraft, which I dared to do one Sunday afternoon. We left Tollerton airfield just outside Nottingham and I was amazed that the 'crooked spire' could be seen from as far away as Hucknall, which goes to prove what a prominent feature the church is within the borough. The other guiding light within the town, seen from the air, was the red, 'crinkly tin' shed roof of B&Q!

As with most towns and organisations, Chesterfield has undergone constant change and development. From the initial Roman settlement onwards, sudden growth spurts have been followed by more stable periods of consolidation. The town is lucky in that it missed much of the postwar building boom of the 1950s and 1960s, when architects were building everything in concrete. We do not have many of their buildings, thankfully; those we have now appear as 'sores' on the town's façades.

In recent years, however, development has caught up rapidly, as the borough has had to adapt to the changing face of industry, transportation and the requirements of the twenty-first century. The pace of change is shown by the inclusion of a number of 'intermediate' photographs between 'Then' and 'Now', mostly taken in the 1960s and '70s, a time with which many readers will still be acutely familiar.

Apart from the 'crinkly tin' developments on the periphery, the redevelopments of the Market Hall, Low Pavement and Vicar Lane have all been completed in styles that are not unsympathetic with the rest of the town. This is a tribute to the local developers and the planning department. Another reason for change has been, of course, to accommodate the car, with the building of the inner relief road and parking facilities. Where the car is concerned, sympathy does not come into it.

As mentioned by Geoff Sadler in *Chesterfield: History and Guide*, the town was 'strangled' within its borough boundary until 1891, when this was extended and space became available to expand and develop. This allowed work to start on new sewers, a mains water supply and other basic items that we take for granted these days. The Victorian entrepreneurs of the time also expanded and enlarged their industries, which were for many years the basis of the town's prosperity.

The heavy industries and the coal mining areas around are now all gone or declining, but new industries are taking their place, and in that category we must include retailing and leisure. White-collar industry is also growing, both in the service sector and IT-related companies, as computers have become a vital part of any commercial enterprise, as well as in the home. This is evident in the large number of office complexes that have grown up and have been filled in the town centre.

I have enjoyed putting all of the photographs together for this book and I hope that it will give you as much, if not more, enjoyment, being able to compare the old with the new. In bringing back memories of the Chesterfield of yesterday I hope I have also created something of a record of the present, useful perhaps to future authors exploring Chesterfield 'Then and Now'.

Brian Davis
January 2003

1

Historic Chesterfield

The parish church, commonly known as the 'crooked spire' owing to its most obvious characteristic, properly St Mary and All Saints Parish Church, dominates the town of Chesterfield. The spire is 9ft out of vertical and is the highest point in the town centre. The church, seen here in 1910, is listed, so it has not altered over the years, and many of the surrounding buildings have also survived.

In 1910 (see page 7), there was a railed enclosure on the west side of the church, known as the Alpine Gardens. This has been opened up to create space within the town. The long-awaited new Information Centre finally opened in December 2002.

The view of the parish church and crooked spire from St Mary's Gate is frequently the one first seen by travellers. I was nearly run over by vehicles getting the 'now' shot, which is quite different from the conditions existing in the 1910s, when children were running around happily in the road. The Anchor Hotel on the right was rebuilt in 1923 and the upper part of the road has not altered substantially since the 1970s (middle photograph) although the use of the buildings may change when the office block is sold.

The Revolution House at Old Whittington is famous for being the alehouse, then called the Cock & Pynot, where the earl of Devonshire, the earl of Danby and Mr John D'Arcy met to plan the overthrow of King James II in 1688. The house is now a museum, but the public house behind carries on the name of the alehouse, though it now uses the modern form of pynot, the magpie (Cock & Magpie). The top picture shows the alehouse frontage when it was rendered; this was removed in 1910. The small inset picture is of a rifleman – the cottage was occupied by the Medieval Society for the 300th anniversary of the original meeting.

No photographic record of Chesterfield would be complete without the town's oldest pub, the Royal Oak, which was known to exist in 1772. It is located in the area known as thr Shambles, and is perhaps one of the oldest in the country. The area around the pub has been opened up, with the overhanging parts of other buildings being removed, possibly owing to their great antiquity.

The Peacock Heritage Centre is now the new Tourist Information Centre near the parish church opens. The building is believed to originate from 1500 and is thought to have been a public hall until 1680, after which it became a domestic house, then in 1929 it was converted into a public house. It was only discovered that it was timber-framed after a fire in the building in 1974. It was restored in 1981 and the upper floor has become the home to exhibitions from local societies for many years.

2
Central Area

Chesterfield Market Place, *c.* 1910.

The central area of Chesterfield revolves around the Market Hall, which has survived from 1857 – although renovated in 1980 when the dome on the tower was replaced with a new fibreglass copy. At the same time the building was extended at the rear, and is again a magnificent centrepiece to the market square.

The market square has changed substantially on the north side, although the market stalls, which are such a feature of the bustling town centre, have been here for at least a century. The changes from the 1970s are less pronounced, with MacFisheries being absorbed into the M&S store. The colourful canopies to the market stalls add brightness to the current scene. The façades of today's buildings to the north side are more utility-orientated than those in the view from about 1910, when the square was more varied and interesting.

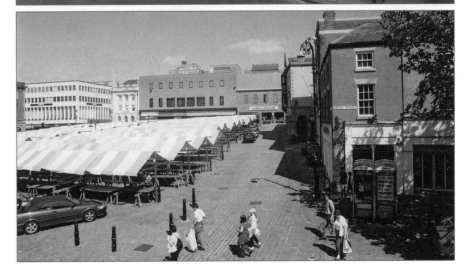

Another interesting corner of the market square is the south-eastern, shown in this sequence of pictures. The buildings have not been altered in plan or elevation although their use has changed. Looking at the upper floors, the window patterns have been maintained although they may have been rebuilt, as the painted walls of Wakefields in the 1970s could not possibly have been cleaned to the standard of the brickwork of the Abbey National. The LloydsTSB building is essentially as it was. Both buildings have been altered only up to the fascia level – but most shoppers never look above the signs.

High Street shows many changes from the 1910s to the present day. The line of the buildings has remained and there is now a complete lack of canopies, alas. They improved the appearance of the street. The large high street multiple stores with their universal façades now dominate the southern side.

New Square, *c.* 1910.

The western side of the Market Hall is another square, this time New Square, and the vibrant market stalls dominate this area. The tram lines first installed in 1904 have long gone, as has the traffic, as it is now a completely traffic-free zone and an excellent public area where Morris dancers and similar groups often perform on summer weekends. Another feature is the number of trees that have been added to the square, which break up the harsh brick façades of the buildings.

Above, the same view in about 1970, and below, 2002.

The post office has stood on the north side of High Street for over 100 years, although it has been extended by taking over part of the Angel Hotel, with its archway for coaches and horses. The remaining part of the Angel site is occupied by the adjacent bank. The hotel site originally extended through to Saltergate and was a very large one. The cobbled road is clearly seen in original and current views. The street scene has substantially improved with the litter bins and flowers from the rather plain street scene of the older two pictures. The view down to the crooked spire is clearly seen in the older images.

The corner of New Square is now overshadowed by trees, with Archbishop Secker's House on the north side now in use as offices and Radio Sheffield. The west side has been rebuilt, although still occupied by Dents the Chemists, now selling a wider range of goods and including a photographic department.

West Bars looking towards the town centre with the Market Hall as backdrop. The electric trams are in full operation, although the horse-drawn cab is still available, both being replaced by the 'horseless carriage'. The older picture shows the old Sun Inn building, rebuilt in 1914 to the terracotta-faced building we know today. The Portland Hotel is still a hostelry, although it has changed to a Wetherspoon's public house.

West Bars looking west from the town centre away from the Market Hall. The old Market Place station of the Lancashire, Derbyshire & East Coast Railway has been replaced – initially with a Post Office building, which has itself now been replaced by the latest Consignia office block. The Portland Hotel and Dents remain, although the chemist's had a new store built in the 1970s.

Further along West Bars the north side of the road has remained, although the uses of the buildings have altered substantially over the years. In 1895 there are baskets hanging outside the tall building and Nadin, who took many of the 'Then' photographs in this book, occupied this building. He had a basket and tobacco shop and took photographs, which he sold as postcards in his shop. In the 1979 shot it has been taken over as the Army recruiting office and it is a hairdressing salon today. The replaced Post Office building can be clearly seen.

Leading back into the town is South Street, whose northern section has continued to change over the years. The 1960s-style concrete building originally built for Fine Fare was later taken over by Wilkinson's and recently extended. At the same time, the Vicar Lane development was constructed, into the part occupied at one time by Rowells and later Fads. The renovated units have remained unlet. The west side of the street has been renovated and is occupied by small shop units. In the 1970s Britt's occupied the shop, a traditional ironmonger with boxes on racks in many rooms, and no stock catalogue other than the proprietor's memory. Quite different from today's DIY 'sheds'.

Looking south along South Street from the bottom of the previous photograph, the road has remained, with the Bowling Green on the right hand side. Beetwell Hall was replaced in the late 1800s with the building shown, which has been occupied since 1938 by Yeomans, the camping and army stores.

The change in the Post Office building is very clearly seen in this pair of photographs. The 1950s-style concrete edifice, with its low, flat-roofed outbuildings, has been swept away for a much more sympathetic building. The foreground brick and asbestos-roofed structures all remain, still in part occupied by the motor trade. The domestic building and garden still maintains its lonely presence within the central area while all around has changed.

Beetwell Street has changed substantially over the years. The old police station and fire station were both demolished in the 1980s. When the new police station was built further along the street, the fire service was relocated to Whittington Moor. The Central Library, a building that has received several design awards, now occupies the site. It is a community facility that the borough should use and be proud of.

Moving along Beetwell Street, to the east the small shops and public houses have been replaced with large modern structures. To the south, the new police headquarters dominates the street – dwarfing another concrete and brick structure, which at one time housed a motor retailer and bowling alley. The north side is the car park to the new Vicar Lane development, which shows how the car tends to dominate the current town scene.

We do not have to go back many years for a street frontage to alter considerably. The north side of Beetwell Street for several years had temporary shops in a raised walkway, which were originally erected to relocate businesses disrupted by the Low Pavement redevelopment, as shown by the 1990 picture. With the reconstruction of the new Vicar Lane development they have been replaced with a multi-storey car park, which has quite a pleasant exterior in keeping with the rest of the development

A part of the town where only the name remains is Vicar Lane, both sides having been demolished, and it is now part of the latest development. The only point of reference in both images is the half-timbered building, the Falcon Restaurant at the end of Low Pavement, and the irregular roofscape of what is now the Pizza Restaurant. The garage on the right-hand side was Kennings, where I tried out a new Ford Capri but unfortunately I was too tall for it: my head caught on the roof lining.

The junction of Low Pavement with South Street is another area that changed substantially over the years – although one building, the Falcon Restaurant, is still there. Low Pavement was originally closed off, but was opened up in the 1920s, the Commercial Hotel being demolished in the early 1970s for the building of Fine Fare, now occupied by Wilkinson's. Vicar Lane was developed in 1934 with the bus station at the end. The building next to Fine Fare had the Grosvenor Rooms on the upper floors, where small receptions and annual dinners of organisations were held. This was demolished to make way for the new shopping development.

Above, the same view in about 1970, and below, 2002.

St James's Hall, part of the parish church complex, was a meeting place known to many over the years as The Settlement. This was another victim of the new Vicar Lane development, the newly relocated Woolworths store being in the vicinity of the old hall. The old 'Woolies' off High Street was also demolished for the new shopping precinct.

The Old Ship Inn stood by St Mary's Gate until 1887. The replacement building was itself replaced in 1922 but had disappeared by 1979, overshadowed by the utilitarian bus station and the temporary shops. The area has been renovated as part of the Vicar Lane development and is now the rear of the BHS department store. It forms a pleasing junction with Beetwell Street, although it is one of the back elevations.

Stephenson Place has remained in use as a road although it was redeveloped early in the twentieth century. The City House has been replaced with the irregularly shaped but imposing bank, which has changed its ownership over the years. The pillar box on the corner that remained there from the early photograph disappeared only recently; a shame, as many are now being listed.

Traffic still moves along Knifesmithgate towards Church Square and the tower on the half-timbered building at the end of the road is still there. The shoe shop of W. Tinley & Son is another retailer that stayed in the same location until recently, when the building was taken over by a charity shop. Fast food outlets are also encroaching on the north side, another new and growing form of retailing. The half-timbered building on the north side originally housed the Gaumont cinema, ballroom and billiard rooms. It became a supermarket, and was broken up into an indoor market.

The 'brutalist' architecture of the 1950s and '60s is clearly shown in this pair of photographs. The 1924 shot shows the demolition of the building for the High Street Vaults (now the Golden Fleece public house) to be built when Knifesmithgate was extended to the Town Hall area. The reconstruction was very much in keeping with the surroundings. Along came the 'conceptual' architects of the 1950s to pull down the buildings and put up the concrete 'sore' that is already beginning to decay.

Perhaps the saddest pictures of all. The eastern end of Saltergate, once one of the medieval streets of the town, was the location of the almshouses. These and the adjacent buildings were all swept away to form the open area car park of Holywell Cross, which, in addition, is the location of the weekly car boot sales and the occasional travelling fair, especially at bank holidays.

The current junction of Holywell Cross with the Sheffield Road has completely changed on its south side since the nineteenth century, when the horse and cart trundled along the road towards the junction with Newbold Road. The removal company building was redeveloped as a motor dealership, Cavendish Motors, part of the Kenning group when my wife worked there. As that company retracted, the site buildings were reduced in size, with the filling station being rebuilt. The rest of the site became another open area car park.

Another view from the top of the Holywell Cross car park, this time looking south-east with the food hall of the Co-operative store dominating the current scene. This has taken over the bus park and the range of cottages. The stone building was formerly occupied by Harry Fish the Furrier, a type of clothing that is no longer acceptable and fashionable other than to the super-rich. The cinema and church on the left-hand side are still there.

Holywell Cross looking east. Little has changed since the 1970s, although the main building, formerly the Royal Hospital, has changed into the headquarters of the Kenning Sixt Motors Group. The old post office, the small white building, which is listed, is still in use as a restaurant. It is now dwarfed by the new office complex that has been built behind it. The Sunday car boot sale is featured and the green fields close to Chesterfield are clearly seen.

The Blue Bell Inn has dominated the corner of Cavendish Street with Holywell Cross for over 100 years. The original public house was demolished in the 1930s during the heyday of construction of 'picture houses', and what was the Regal adjoins the current building towards the town centre. This building was erected behind the existing one as part of the overall widening of the streets in that part of the town. The reconstruction of the east side of the junction pre-dates this – although not at first for the present occupiers, who eventually expanded into the building with their enlarged store.

The junction of Holywell Street and Stephenson Place has had Eyre's on the corner for over 100 years. The current building was in existence when S.E. Redfern Ltd had their butcher's shop on the opposite corner. The pickled tongues have gone but the furnisher has remained. The east side has been redeveloped, shops changing ownership with the passing fashions. Clarke's of Retford, dry cleaners, and the specialised tobacconists are no more and the sellers of 45s and LPs have changed to multiple megastores retailing CDs and DVDs.

Saltergate, one of the original medieval roads into the borough, is thought to have obtained its name from the traders carrying salt from Cheshire.
The main building featured consisted of town houses, conveniently sited near the centre.
The building has altered little over the years, although it is now used mainly as offices for professionals.

A building that has not
altered externally over the
last 100 years is the
Stephenson Memorial Hall,
named to commemorate the
father of steam railways,
who died at Tapton House
and is buried only a few
hundred yards from the
hall. The north wing was
added in 1898 but the
name has been altered to
the Pomegranate Theatre
and the far section now
houses the Town Museum.
It previously held the
library until the
construction of the new
central library in 1985.

The view from the church spire looking north-east shows the decline of industry in the town over the last 20 years. Markham's has now disappeared and is being replaced with housing, and the replaced railway station is very visible with its white roof. The roof of Stephenson Memorial Hall fills in the foreground of both pictures on the right, which also show how close the fields and golf course are to the centre of the town.

A further view from the church tower, this time looking south. It clearly shows the substantial increase in traffic. The large concrete structures at the end of Markham Road starkly dominate the scene, while the new Pavements development has harmonised into the town and is only dominant by virtue of its size. The utilitarian omnibus station of the Chesterfield Corporation was clearly no loss to the town scene. The current changing face of the town, with industry giving way to retail, is also seen in the MFI and Carpet World buildings visible in the upper section of the current development.

This is another of the pictures taken from the church tower looking north-west, clearly shows the extent of the clearance that occurred when Holywell Cross car park was created, with substantial road widening, as the town has been adapted to the needs of the motor car. The Blue Bell is in the foreground of both pictures, and the old Royal Hospital is just behind the old church building. It is currently occupied by the YMCA, but will soon be closing down.

3
Shopping

Modern town centres revolve around their retail outlets, and the UK's relatively buoyant economy is being sustained by the current boom in retail sales, stoked by rising house prices. Over the last two decades, retail trading has altered substantially, with out-of-town retail parks (basically industrial units used as large shops) and high-class, prestigious large shopping malls, the idea for which was imported from America. These malls are all covered and background heated in the winter. Town centre shopping of the traditional style has not disappeared, however, and is flourishing in Chesterfield, the new Vicar Lane development having only recently been completed. In the view of the author, it has been built very sympathetically and is an excellent asset to the borough. Thank you, Prince Charles, for making those comments many years ago about traditional architecture!

Elliott's the confectioner had their own factory in the borough near the current location of the HSBC bank. Chesterfield Corporation had organised a shopping festival and Elliott's are displaying their certificate for having been awarded first prize. It is thought that the couple at the shop entrance are Mr and Mrs Elliott. By contrast, below, we have a large number of travel agents in the town selling overseas package holidays – a trade that exploded after the Second World War with the advent of affordable air travel.

Mention has been made of C.H. Nadin, whom we have to thank for taking and producing so many photographs of Chesterfield at around the time of the First World War. His shop was on West Bars and he was primarily a basketmaker and tobacconist. Notice the decorated pilasters at the side of the windows. By contrast, Computer World is selling the product that the government considers will be in everyone's home in the near future.

Jewellers are still with us, as is the pawnbroker with his three brass balls. Some things do not alter. Security is increasingly on all traders' minds, and even more on the insurance companies', who demand all the latest grilles and high security systems. Charles Price was on High Street, possibly in the same building as Stuart Bradley, so there is some continuity here – although the shop did have other uses before being taken over by Mr Bradley. Window displays for this trade have altered little over the years.

This page shows the same pair of buildings again, but its use has altered. It is at the top of the Market Place and Taylor's the General Drapers occupied the shop for many years. It was featured on many photographs taken of the Market Place when the tramlines were being installed. Boots are now in the Low Pavement development in a large store where they still sell 'toiletry requisites'. Drapery has given way to shoes in the corner unit.

These pictures show the contrast in the style of window displays. A. Hunt, Leather and Grindery dealer, attempted to include as many examples as possible of his wares in the one window. By contrast, the current trend of some retailers is to create a simple and eyecatching display.

Some men's tailors still follow tradition by trying to include as large a display of clothing in the window as these photographs indicate. What has changed is the balance of the goods on display. Mr Brown recognised the importance of his hat sales, especially as most people wore hats at that time, and the early scenes in this book show everyone wearing a hat. This fashion has decreased although it appears to be coming back with informal headgear. Only three hats are on display in the later photograph.

Food retailing in these shops remains similar, although the window displays are less crowded. Cleanliness is still as important as it was in the 1910s, though no plastic bags were in evidence at that time!

Shopfronts have altered considerably over the last 100 years. In 1910 they were very ornate, with fancy decorations and sun blinds. Today, the architecture is simple, with the display dominating the façade. Strong colours are used to catch shoppers' attention. Many original façades are still in existence, however, and complement the modern units. The upper windows of shops have also disappeared – they were introduced so that travellers on the top decks of trams would be attracted to the shop.

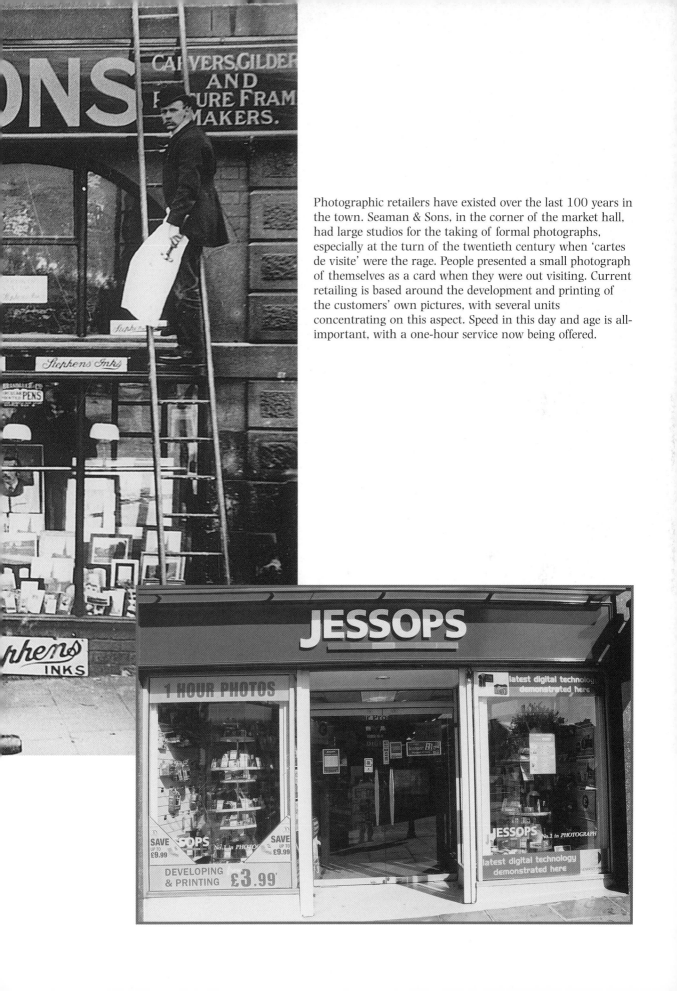

Photographic retailers have existed over the last 100 years in the town. Seaman & Sons, in the corner of the market hall, had large studios for the taking of formal photographs, especially at the turn of the twentieth century when 'cartes de visite' were the rage. People presented a small photograph of themselves as a card when they were out visiting. Current retailing is based around the development and printing of the customers' own pictures, with several units concentrating on this aspect. Speed in this day and age is all-important, with a one-hour service now being offered.

The end of an era, with the closure of haberdashers' shop Brailsford and Way, which occurred during the taking of the current set of photographs. The shop was established in 1890 and, until recently, sewing lessons were given on the upper floors. The original photograph was loaned to the author by the current owners, having been found in a box of papers and photographs. Letters and invoices going back to 1900 were in the box and it is possible that the two ladies in front of the door were the original Misses Brailsford and Way.

The growth of the large, 'crinkly tin' shopping units can clearly be seen in the development of the Riverside Retail Park. These places always seem to be called parks, but for cars rather than humans to take their leisure! The industrial units at the back are still in existence but the open car park has disappeared for the new-style shops. The Wingerworth Carbonisation Plant can be seen romantically on the skyline.

Another pair showing the Riverside Retail Park, this time with the concrete block of Derbyshire County Council's Community Service Centre dominating the foreground. The footbridge over Markham Road disappeared with the new park, and the bus station has lost all of its covered roofs. The bus station is little used, as most buses now pick up passengers at the rear of the Central Pavements development.

Another casualty of the Riverside Retail Park was the Queen's Park Hotel, which survived from 1913 when it was built as part of the Markham Road construction on the corner with Park Road. It lost its battle with the car when it became part of the car park to the shops. Most of the pub site is now a flowerbed.

Thanks to EU regulations, which require the presence of a qualified vet to supervise the slaughter of animals, somewhat against their nature it might be thought, the changing face of industry now includes a substantial reduction in the number of licensed abattoirs in the countryside. Chesterfield had one, but that too was swept away with the Riverside Retail Park. It closed initially for the first stage of development, but the rest of the site was lost with the current extension and it never reopened.

4

Hospitals

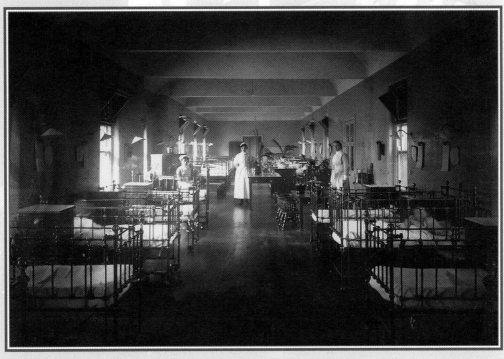

Maternity ward at Chesterfield Royal Hospital, 1917.

Ashgate Hospital was used by the Royal Hospital as a unit for looking after the terminally ill. The main entrance was photographed a few days before it closed with the patients being transferred to the new site at Calow. The building has since been taken over by a charity running the Ashgate Hospice and it has been enlarged and modernised.

With the building of the new hospital at Calow in 1982/3, Scarsdale Hospital, as it was known in later years, the Union Hospital on this Nadin postcard closed. This was where many Chesterfield citizens first saw the light of day as the maternity unit was on the top floor. It stood empty for many years and was finally demolished in 2001 to make way for the current residential development.

Chesterfield's Royal Hospital has dominated the north-east side of Holywell Street (later Holywell Cross) for over 100 years, and has a most imposing façade. Following closure as a hospital, it stood empty for many years while most of the surrounding buildings were demolished, until in the 1980s it was taken over by the Kenning Group for their headquarters. Extended and modernised, it remains an attractive building. The new building at Calow is a major asset to the town and its surrounding area, and has a prominent entrance. Car parking, however, is still a major problem around the hospital; the NHS never seems to get this right.

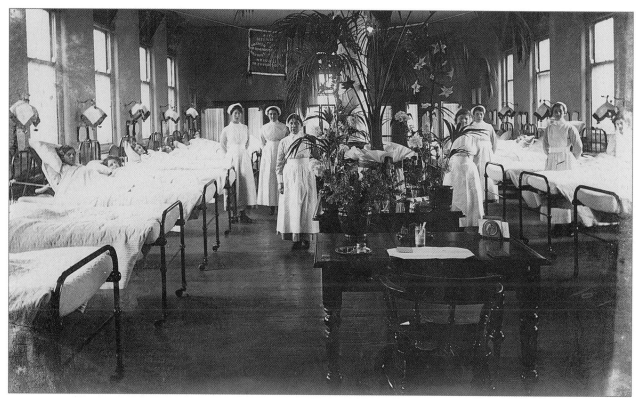

The large wards of the old Royal Hospital have now disappeared into six-bed units within the new hospital. The high-tech arrangements of the modern hospital are evident when compared with 1917, when gaslights were provided over each bed. The aspidistras have now disappeared and the hospital staff's uniform is more informal.

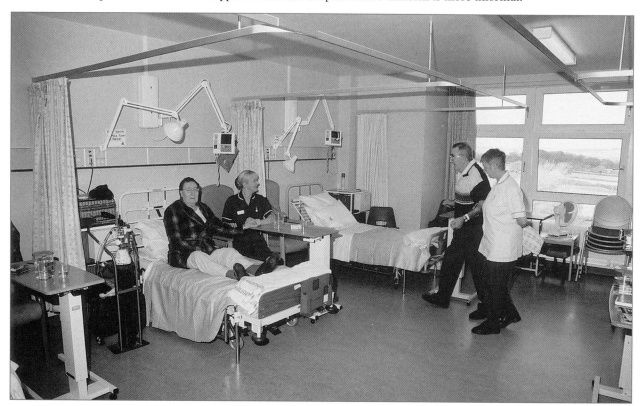

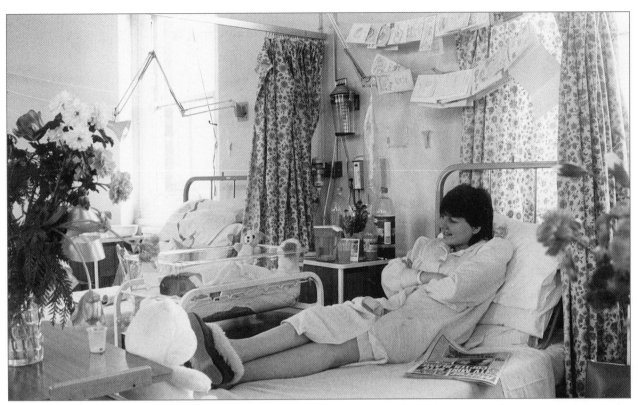

Most people start their life these days in the hospital maternity unit. In 1917 (as seen in the picture on p. 69) the obstetrics ward was sternly formal but the modern maternity unit is light and airy. The 1980s shot was taken only a few weeks before the town centre unit transferred to its current site, each section again being in small divisions off a central hub.

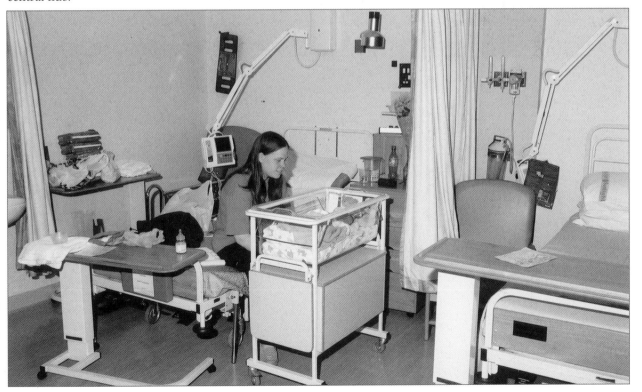

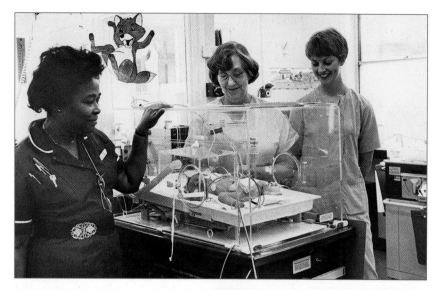

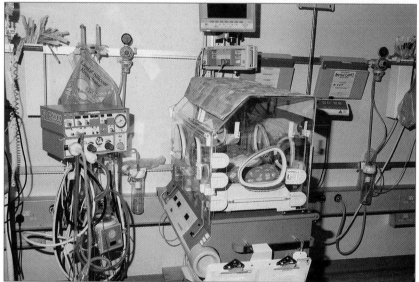

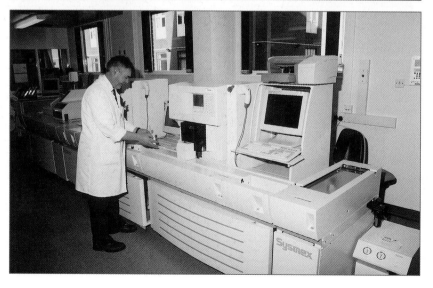

The special care unit for premature babies has in recent years become a high-tech operation. The increase in the use of equipment is shown in the two units over less than 20 years. As with all the hospital departments they are backed up with even more high-tech equipment in the pathology department, such as the diagnostic machine (left).

5

People & Pleasure

A wedding party in the early years of the twentieth century.

A town or city is all about the people who live, love and die there. Weddings are an important part of any person's life and have been recorded in photographs from the start of the medium. What has changed is the style of dress and the now generally more informal nature of the photographic record, as seen here.

With any wedding there are also the group photographs. The record of the gathering of all the friends and relatives has always been a mandatory part of the proceedings. The interest is all in the dress and styles of the wedding group.

Queen's Park with its large green areas has been the open space of the town following dedication in 1887 and its opening in 1893. The River Rother, which once separated the area from the developments, has now been culverted and trees completely obscure the town centre from the park. Queen's Park is still used for cricket, although county matches are no longer played there since the redevelopment of the county ground at Derby. The park is also the home of the town's garden nursery, and the flower beds are always well maintained. In the Nadin photograph (above) the Lancashire & East Coast Railway can be seen, as well as part of the station.

The footbridge connecting the park with West Bars in the town centre has always been an important link. The 1982 image clearly shows how the old Post Office block dominated the view. This could not now be repeated as the trees have grown higher and the new Consignia building is not so tall. The 'now' photograph therefore had to be taken from the bridge, at about the middle of the River Rother.

Over the years, Chesterfield has maintained a bandstand in the park. The current one has been restored by the Borough and is still used to entertain during the summer months.

The boating lake in Queen's Park is as popular today as it was in 1907. The 'then' picture is from a coloured postcard made by G. Marsden & Sons of Wirksworth. In the summer months the boats still are in regular use. A miniature railway (inset) also runs around the lake.

Another popular pastime is wandering around Chesterfield's market and car boot sales. Market Place was quite substantial even on the maps of 1803 and it continues to be a centre of attraction on market days. Health regulations have stopped many items being sold, like the kippers in the 1910 photograph above. Nevertheless it still does a good trade as CDs and similar items now replace the kippers. Sunday is the day for car boot sales at Holywell Cross and these are always well attended by sellers and buyers alike.

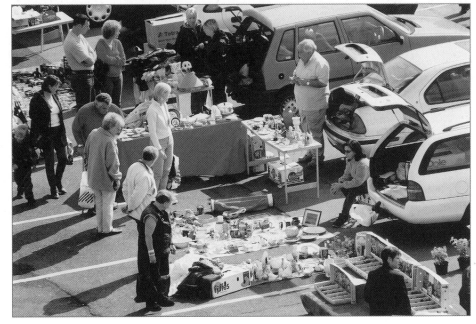

Chesterfield Bowling Green is reputed to date from the fourteenth century and still has a very active membership, although the attire of the participants has greatly altered over the years.

The interior of the Portland Hotel has seen drastic changes over the last few years. Until recently the interior construction had not changed from the time of the original 1910s photograph, although the fittings had. When Wetherspoon's took over they removed all of the front dividing walls to create a large open-plan area, which is used for the purchase of food as well as drinks. Otherwise, the company is known for its sensitivity in maintaining the original character of the buildings it takes over.

Fairs visit the town from time to time, especially at bank holiday times, and it is interesting to compare the styles of two helter-skelters, still a popular attraction, although the two photographs are nearly 100 years apart. The modern unit now collapses down to be towed on a trailer, rather than being a sectional unit, which required many hours for erection and dismantling.

The canal has altered from a working environment to one used entirely for pleasure. The Canal Society has rebuilt many locks and restored a great length of waterway and Derbyshire County Council has completely rebuilt the lock keeper's cottage as a 'Countryside Ranger' station, which also sells drinks, food and tourist trinkets. The boat in the lock is used for giving pleasure rides.

The local army regiment is the Sherwood Foresters, and they have the right to march through the borough with bayonets fixed and swords drawn. They last exercised this right in September 2002. They also marched through the town in 1909, when they had new colours.

The old courthouse stood on Beetwell Street, backing on to the bowling green. This was replaced in 1965 by the book-shaped building in West Bars, which has four courts. Business continued to expand and currently the building on St Mary's Gate, which used to be the Labour Exchange, is now the County Court with the West Bars building being used as a Magistrates Court. This is again soon to alter with a new court building under construction on Durrant Road. The fate of the West Bars building, which has roof problems, is unknown, although it is listed.

One of the requirements that planning authorities can enforce is that 1 per cent of the cost of a development over £1m has to be spent on 'works of art'. With the Post Office building, currently Consignia and soon to be renamed the Post Office again, they commissioned sculptures from Dame Barbara Hepworth. The original work, seen in 1990 in front of the old building, has been relocated to the opposite side of the bridge from the town centre to Queen's Park. Well done Chesterfield Planning for insisting on that clause being enforced! Sculptures of any type help to break up an otherwise mundane street scene.

Under 'pleasure', I have also included the long-vanished Brampton Brewery, as their products gave pleasure to many over the years. The building stood until 1984, although beer had not been brewed there since 1955. The site is now occupied by the B&Q store. Dare I mention pleasure and DIY in the same breath?

The Crown Hotel was situated on Lordsmill Street, and was demolished in 1966 to make way for the bowling alley and nightclub complex. This also included on the ground floor a Chinese restaurant, which still remains, although its name has changed. It was always a friendly place, considering the Crown Hotel had grilles on the bars to protect the staff, and they served the drinks through the gaps in the bars.

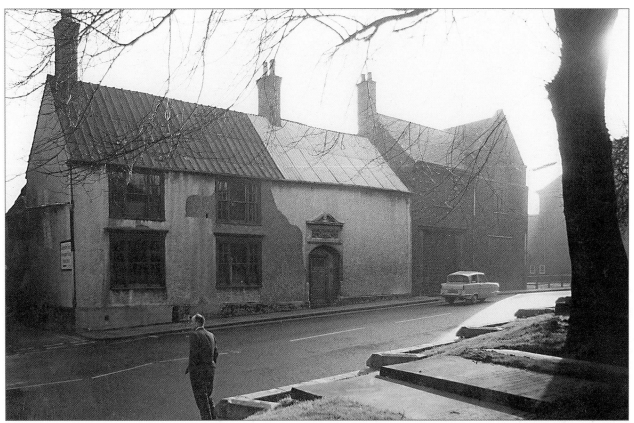

It is always good to see a building that has been renovated with care and is well used. Such is Gilbert Heathcote's house on St Mary's Gate. He was a wealthy merchant trading with Spain and Jamaica, who assisted in founding the Bank of England in 1694. His house is listed and used for pleasure as a bar and restaurant, and previous neglect has been reversed.

It was inevitable that a public house would be named after the famous crooked spire. The first was in Church Lane (above) and this was demolished in 1930 for the current building when Church Way was constructed. The new Tourist Information Centre now dominates the road and the public house has changed its name to the Slug & Fiddle.

Another public house substantially altered over the years is the Punch Bowl, with its highly decorative front. This was originally the Turf Tavern and the new building was built behind the existing one in 1931 when Holywell Street was widened before it was demolished. The original photograph has been heavily restored as it was in two pieces and very degraded.

6

Horn's Bridge

I have included this as a separate section as Horn's Bridge was one of the main entry points to the town centre, and has substantially altered over the years.

The junction of all the roads at the south of Chesterfield was also the crossing point for all three railway lines serving the town. All but the Midland Main Line have vanished, and the road has been diverted to the other side of the factory building. The road shown is now a dead end.

The junction viewed from the south clearly showed the imposing brick arches of the Lancashire, Derbyshire & East Coast Railway. While they were not used for many years, they did remain partly demolished for a time. By the junction for many years stood the Horn's Hotel, which closed in 1970. It is not known if the hotel was named after the bridge or vice versa.

A pair of photographs taken from the footbridge over the end of the bypass, which shows clearly the decline of traditional industry and the increase in leisure. Bryan Donkin's factory on the west side has reduced in size and the Tube Works on the east has completely disappeared, in favour of eating houses, cinema and fitness buildings.

The view over the Horn's Bridge island looking towards the town has been considerably tidied up over the last 20 years. Relics of the old railways have been removed and in accordance with current practice a 'forest' is developing within the island.

Flooding is not new at Horn's Bridge, these floods halted all traffic in November 2001, but checking through old photographic records reveals that similar floods have occurred many times in that area over the years. Nothing alters.

7

Transport

The Great Central Railway station under construction, *c.* 1890. The Inner Relief Road was
built on the line of the Great Central Railway. The line lasted until the Beeching era and closed
in 1967.

The road was built in 1985 and is now an important part of the road system of the town. The trees lining it are getting large and in the summer months they hide the industry to the east of the road.

The first railway station in Chesterfield was built by the Midland Railway in 1868. Part of this survives in the insurance office just by the entrance to the current forecourt of the station, having been moved from its original location beside the line. Today Chesterfield is blessed with a 'modern' railway station.

This spread and overleaf: The movement of people has always been an important feature of any town and, until deregulation, Chesterfield Borough Council was the main carrier. The horse-drawn cart with seats was operated by private carrier, here seen outside the Devonshire Hotel, date unknown. The Corporation initially had horse-drawn trams on rails until, in 1904, the electric tram arrived. These lasted until 1927, when the trolley bus replaced them; however, their death knoll had been sounded as, at the same time, the motor bus arrived. This has developed into the sleek, customer-friendly, low-line buses of today. However, a Chesterfield tram still runs and carries passengers at the National Tramway Museum at Crich.

8
Surrounding Districts

Chatsworth Road, one of the main arterial routes out of town, is travelled both by citizens of the borough and those passing through. About one mile out of the centre the road divides, with Old Road going off to the right towards Brampton and the main road towards the Peak District. The junction has lost that elegant, tall building, which at one time was the local police station, although in the 1910s it appears to have been a house.

One end of the tramway was in Whittington Moor. Still visited by the local buses, it is also the terminus of the inner relief road, at the island in the background of the current picture. The buildings to the east side still remain today.

Turning around from the previous pair of photographs, and looking towards the town again, the street façades have not altered greatly from the view on the postcard above, which was posted in Chesterfield in 1943 – although the picture appears to originate from an earlier time.

Chesterfield from Spital Green
24/8 24

On the eastern side of the town is Spital, said to have taken its name from a leper hospital. Substantially domestic as shown in the old pencil drawing, the area was occupied by Markham's and was the birthplace of the tunnelling machine used to drill the Channel Tunnel, but that has now all gone and housing again is filling the area. The office block with all the scaffolding around it is listed and is currently being altered.

These photographs taken over a three-year interval from the church tower, show how the industrial buildings of Markham's have all gone and new housing is quickly filling the space. The pictures show how close the green fields are to the centre of the town. The mass of trees on the right-hand side of both pictures is the Spital cemetery.

Another set of pictures showing the decline of industry in the area, with the large industrial cranes in the 1940s reduced to low-level industrial buildings in 1977 and to housing in 2002. The changing skyline of the town is also visible.

The changing skyline of the town is once more clearly seen in these pictures taken from the golf course on the hill towards Calow. The 1904 image is from a coloured postcard of that time and many of the buildings are still in existence in 1977. Then the dramatic alterations of the past twenty years can be seen in the present-day picture.

The ornamental fountain, which graced New Square for many years, is actually greatly travelled. It started its life in Eastwood Park at Hasland and was a feature in the opening ceremony in 1913. It was then moved to New Square and was a feature there until 2001, when it was returned to its old home.

A short distance away from the fountain and adjacent to the local shopping area is The Green, another area where the buildings existing in 1908 still survive today, although their former use was mainly domestic with the proverbial corner shop, and is now changed to a row of retail and light industrial premises.

9
Outlying Areas

The old church at Wingerworth dates from the thirteenth century. The exterior is little altered other than for the removal of the ivy, which was much loved by the Victorians but in fact did no good at all to the structure of the building.

All Saints' parish church, Wingerworth, 2002.

Internally, the old nave in Wingerworth church, seen above in the 1910s, has been well preserved and is now used as the assembly point for the new nave. This has been added in a modernist style to create an airy and greatly admired interior. While the two styles contrast, they complement each other harmoniously, showing that not all modern developments need be nostalgically designed.

On the outskirts of Wingerworth, on the south side of the borough boundary, was the Carbonisation Plant, built on the site of Ryknield Street, the Roman road. The plant closed a few years ago and the clearance of the contaminated land is the subject of a four-year reclamation scheme. Work started in 2001 and the plant, seen here in its heyday of 1980, was reduced to several structures by July 2002, when the later photograph was taken on an open day. Those buildings have now all gone and the remaining tower is due to be demolished early in 2003.

The Bull's Head Inn in Holymoorside remains a very popular pub by the crossroads in the village – although the method of transportation has greatly altered. The cotton mills in the background have now disappeared and the area has more tree cover.

The village school has altered little from the old picture, taken in about 1915, to the present day, although at the time of the later picture the school had closed and may be up for sale. The building was then hidden from the road by trees. The children of the village have transferred to a new school, which incorporates energy-saving measures such as solar panels and rainwater tanks for flushing the toilets. The houses at the bottom of the street are still there, more having been built.

Many of the changes illustrated previously are seen from these aerial shots. The loss of the rectory grounds for the new Vicar Lane development is clearly seen, as well as the scale of the centre. Both pictures show the dominant position of St Mary's Church in the borough, and I was especially favoured on my recent flight in a small, single-engine aeroplane when a shaft of sunshine lit up the church as we flew over. The stalls in the market square are clearly seen at the bottom left of the picture.

Another of my recent aerial shots contrasts greatly with one taken in the 1960s. This time it is the West Bars area, where the small gasholder in the bottom right has gone and is replaced by the large Bingo hall on the opposite side of the road to B&Q. The Brampton Brewery can be seen where B&Q now stands. The older image very clearly shows the old layout of Queen's Park before the building of the swimming pool, while the River Rother is also easily seen, running parallel between the road and park.

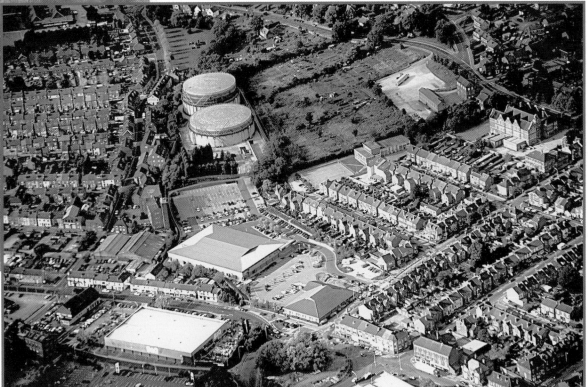

The final pair of aerial shots is of the Horn's Bridge area, and these show the substantial alteration that has been made to cater for the car. In both shots the railway line crosses the bottom left-hand side of the image, and in the 1960s picture a goods trains can be clearly seen. The construction of the roundabout and the loss of heavy industry to the leisure industry is shown to the west of the Midland line. MFI also stands partly on the site of the row of cottages.

ACKNOWLEDGEMENTS

Acknowledgements are always difficult, not so much for who you include but for the constant thought of who you have forgotten. Firstly, I must thank my old friend and colleague David Roberts, who introduced me to collecting magic lanterns and slides. He and I travelled around for many years together, giving shows. This stopped only when he 'emigrated' to Lancashire. David has generously given me access to his extensive collection of photographs of old Chesterfield. Geoff Sadler kindly helped me to check my historical facts. My thanks are also owed to the staff of the Chief Executive's office, and to the nurses and staff of Chesterfield Royal Hospital, who made me most welcome. Dave Guilor safely flew me over the town, and Mel Hardy expertly restored the old photograph of the Punch Bowl pub on page 96.

For other photographs my thanks go to:

Roy Thompson, Malcolm Sales of Buttercross Photography, Anne Krawszik of the local studies section of the Chesterfield Library, Ken Davis, Chesterfield Photographic Society, Mr Crossley of Brailsford & Wray.

Finally, my thanks to the many others who gave me help and assistance.